Original title:
Ballads of the Bracken

Copyright © 2025 Creative Arts Management OÜ
All rights reserved.

Author: Natalia Harrington
ISBN HARDBACK: 978-1-80567-339-2
ISBN PAPERBACK: 978-1-80567-638-6

Hymn of the Honeysuckle Wind

In the garden the bees do dance,
A waltz of nectar, a sweet romance.
With every buzz, a giggle near,
The flowers whisper, "Bring us cheer!"

The breeze it tickles, a playful tease,
Tickling noses and rustling leaves.
A dandelion dreams, it takes to flight,
Spreading wishes with pure delight.

Shadows on the Shaded Trail

Frolicsome squirrels chase each other,
One leaps high, then falls like butter.
A shadow flits, is it a sprite?
Or just a rogue leaf taking flight?

The path is lined with giggling gnomes,
Who whisper secrets of far-off homes.
Their tiny boots make nary a sound,
As they dance around, all merry and brown.

Memories of the Meadow's Edge

A cow mooed loud, it told a joke,
While high above, the buzzards spoke.
They laughed and flapped their wings so wide,
As daisies swayed with utmost pride.

The rabbits hop with a comic flair,
Wearing carrots like hats, haute-couture wear.
Each leap a laugh, each wiggle a grin,
In this sunny patch, where the fun begins.

Twilight in the Thicket

As twilight paints the sky in hues,
The fireflies start their silly ruse.
They flash their lights like mischievous sprites,
Dancing around in frolicsome flights.

The nightingale sings a tune quite absurd,
A serenade that's never heard.
With every note a chuckle breaks,
In this thicket of giggles, where joy awakes.

The Serenity of the Shaded Refuge

In the shade where squirrels dance,
A bumblebee lost in a trance.
With acorns falling all around,
A giggle echoes, quite profound.

Leaves whisper secrets up above,
While chatting squirrels talk of love.
A picnic mat does sway and dip,
As snacks are stolen—what a trip!

The sun peeks in, a cheeky glance,
While ants parade as if they prance.
Laughter bursts like bubbles in air,
In this refuge, lighter than care.

Caress of the Canopied Glimpse

Underneath the leafy fold,
Stories of mischief are told.
A chipmunk's stash goes missing fast,
While all his friends are laughing past.

The sunlight spots a dancing leaf,
That twirls and spins—oh, what a thief!
It steals away the quiet plays,
As shadows sway in silly ways.

With laughter brewing like hot tea,
The forest seems alive with glee.
Creatures pause to joke and jest,
In the canopy, they feel their best.

The Allure of Autumn's Abandon

Crisp leaves tumble, twirl, and spin,
With laughter echoing beneath the din.
Pumpkin hats the squirrels declare,
As they leap from here to there.

Ghostly whispers of cider sweet,
As critters dance on little feet.
In every nook, mischief ignites,
With scarecrows joining silly fights.

Golden sunsets paint the sky,
As tangled vines swing low and high.
In this abandon, joy we find,
With every chuckle, hearts unwind.

Promenade through the Pollen Pathways

Bumblebees buzz like tiny drums,
While flowers gossip of their chums.
Marching ants in a silly rush,
Stumble over stems in a hush.

Pollen drifts like fairy dust,
Creating giggles on the gust.
Bees wear hats, so jaunty and tall,
As they trip over blooms and fall.

Through pathways bright with colors bold,
Nature's canvases unfold.
With every step, a chuckle's shared,
In this parade, no heart is scared.

Chronicles Beneath the Cattails

In the glade where frogs take the stage,
A chorus of croaks, a wild rampage.
The ducks wear top hats, strut with flair,
While turtles giggle without a care.

A raccoon juggles shiny bright rocks,
And squirrels plot mischief with sneaky stocks.
The fireflies dance in a dazzling glow,
As the moon winks down on the lively show.

Beneath the reeds, a gossiping breeze,
Whispers of folly that never cease.
The otters slide down a slippery spree,
Creating a ruckus, oh such glee!

So grab your boots and join the chase,
In this merry wood, there's no time to waste.
For laughter awaits in the soft, green patch,
Where stories of whimsy are born to hatch.

Echoing Heartbeats in the Underbrush

In the thickets where the critters play,
A babbling brook sings all day.
The badgers tell tales of gigantic pies,
While hummingbirds swoop to catch the flies.

There's a hedgehog with a dapper bow tie,
Who tells the worst jokes that make you sigh.
A family of mice hosts a tea party,
But serves acorns, oh so hearty!

The laughter erupts like a bubbling spring,
As the chipmunks dance and the rabbits sing.
Fireflies flutter like thoughts in flight,
Illuminating the wild, enchanting night.

And if you listen, you'll surely hear,
The echo of joy that's always near.
In this bright thicket, with mirth and cheer,
The heartbeats of fun are crystal clear.

Gaze into the Grove's Heart

In the grove where shadows prance,
A squirrel sings, a tree branches dance,
Laughter echoes through the green,
As flowers giggle, unseen, obscene.

The wind whispers, tickles the leaves,
A wise old owl, or so he believes,
Winks at a rabbit, bold and spry,
Who takes a leap, then wonders why.

Bees in bow ties, buzzing about,
With honey jokes that leave no doubt,
The mushrooms sway in posh attire,
While foxes joke, their jokes never tire.

So gaze into the grove's bright heart,
A whimsical scene, a work of art,
Where nature's humor finds its way,
Turning the mundane into play.

Adrift in the Acanthus

In the weeds, oh what a sight,
A snail in shoes, a comical plight,
With every inch, he takes a leap,
While nearby ants hold a grand sweep.

The thorns wear hats upon their tips,
As butterflies gather for sweet sips,
Sip and slide on nectar rides,
While frogs croak out their rhyming guides.

A hedgehog spins a tale so bold,
Of adventures lost in marzipan gold,
He points his quills in secretly,
To paint a map of ecstasy.

So ahoy, adrift in green's embrace,
With laughter echoing every space,
We dance amongst the flowering array,
In a world where mirth holds sway.

Nightfall over the Nettle

As sun dips low, a moonrise glow,
The nettles giggle, putting on the show,
A firefly winks, a glowworm hums,
While crickets chirp their evening drums.

Bats in capes flap in delight,
Swooping low, they steal the night,
With shadows cast, a cocktail of fun,
Making mischief till the day is done.

A badger juggles acorns galore,
While frogs recite their rhymes and lore,
Beneath the stars, they dance and spin,
A wild party, where all grin.

So when darkness claims the glade,
Let laughter rise in this escapade,
For nightfall brings a light-hearted tease,
In the nettle's arms, we find our ease.

The Promise of the Sapling

Once a twig with dreams so bright,
A sapling peeks into the light,
Says to the soil, 'I'm quite the catch,'
While worms below play a friendly match.

With each new leaf, a story told,
Of battles fought and treasures sold,
The wind can carry seasons' tune,
Rumbling jokes with a jazzy croon.

A sprinkle of rain turns giggles round,
Bouncing droplets on soft ground,
The sapling stretches, reaching high,
Tickling clouds that drift on by.

So here we stand, with roots so deep,
In laughter's fold, our promise keeps,
For every sapling comes to know,
That life is best when shared in tow.

The Riddle of the Silent Glade

In a glade where whispers creep,
A squirrel swears he'll never sleep.
He claims the owls, with their wise eyes,
Steal all dreams, much to his surprise.

The brook gurgles a cheeky tune,
While frogs hop, dressed for a grand noon.
Tadpoles dance with glee and mirth,
As dragonflies boast of their flight's worth.

A rabbit with a silly grin,
Hops on toes, a dance to win.
He challenges the fox to a race,
Both trip over roots, oh what a chase!

When night falls and stars fray,
The glade has secrets, come what may.
Yet all who wander here will find,
Laughter echoes, one of a kind.

A Symphony of Fern and Feather

A woodpecker taps a jolly beat,
While hedgehogs jig on tiny feet.
The ferns sway and twist in cheer,
As creatures gather for a seer.

With wings that flutter, bees do hum,
While mice join in, their faces dumb.
They sing of honey and of cheese,
Creating chaos, if you please.

An owl shouts, 'Hold your notes!'
But laughter spills and overflows.
Each creature grins, from tiny to tall,
In this concert, joy conquers all.

As twilight dawns with a wink,
The critters stop to chat and think.
In harmony they troop away,
Planning mischief for the next day.

Whimsy of the Woodland Creatures

A raccoon in a top hat struts,
While parading past two silly mutts.
He jokes about his midnight snacks,
And flips his wink with silly facts.

The deer prance in a grand parade,
While boisterous monkeys toss and trade.
They chortle loud, they tell tall tales,
Of slippery slopes and playful trails.

A badger dons some flashy shades,
Shouting out the latest escapades.
He trips and falls, but laughs aloud,
His spirit's high, he stands so proud.

As dusk creeps in, they gather 'round,
To share the fun their day had found.
In woodland's heart, where spirits soar,
Silly antics are never a bore.

Chants of the Wandering Willow

The willow sways with a wrinkled laugh,
Tickling sprites as they dance and quaff.
They prance about, with glee they shout,
 'What's life without a picnic route?'

A critter crew with pies galore,
Share a feast by the old oak door.
A turtle, slow, drops his jelly slice,
And turns to joke, 'This is quite nice!'

A fox invites all to the ball,
With berry juice that flows for all.
They twirl and spin till morning light,
Chasing away the shadows of night.

When dawn breaks, what a sight to see!
The adventure spills with glee and glee.
Under the tree, where laughter flows,
The willow whispers, 'More fun, who knows?"

Fantasies in the Fern-Flecked Isles

In a land where ferns wear hats,
A frog skips past with fancy spats.
He jigs and dances on lily pads,
While muttering jokes and wearing fads.

The crickets laugh and crash a show,
While bees join in, all a-glow.
A snail brings cheese to the feast,
'It's gouda!' he shouts, like a well-fed beast.

Amidst the fun, a turtle sighs,
'I'm late, I'm late!' he loudly cries.
But no one worries, the party's grand,
In fern-filled isles, life is well planned.

So if you wander where green ferns grow,
Expect the odd and the bright-to-glow.
With laughter loud, and joy to share,
In this isle of fancies, without a care.

The Pulse of the Pollen Breeze

A bee with shades and a tiny tie,
Buzzes and dances, oh, my, oh, my!
He tells the flowers, 'You're all the rage!'
While secretly plotting to hit the stage.

The daisies sway in a gentle trance,
As poppies try their best to prance.
A dandelion shouts, 'I'm going pro!'
While butterflies laugh at the pollen flow.

A gust of wind starts a pollen spree,
With all the blooms caught in riotous glee.
'Catch me if you can!' a tulip shouts loud,
While sprinting away, it feels quite proud.

At dusk they gather beneath the trees,
To share the tales of their frolics and fees.
In the pollen breeze, joy has its say,
As flowers giggle and dance the night away.

Secrets Stitched in Silk

A spider spins tales with threads of grace,
While crickets cheer from a cozy place.
They whisper secrets in the night,
Of lost socks and a messy flight.

The caterpillar laughs, all snug in its shell,
'I've lost my way, can you tell?'
But the spider winks, says, 'Take your time,
Each thread is woven in rhythm and rhyme.'

A moth arrives, with style so bold,
'I'm here for this story, if truth be told.'
With each stitch shared, they dance in delight,
Under the moon's soft and silvery light.

So gather round, for the tales are sweet,
Of silken threads and journeys neat.
In the heart of night, they spin and weave,
With laughter and secrets, we all believe.

Legends of the Leafy Labyrinth

In a maze of greenery, bright and wide,
A squirrel seeks treasures and wisdom to guide.
'Are nuts the prize?' he turns in each lane,
'Or is it just acorns that drive me insane?'

A hedgehog shouts, 'Come quick! Come fast!'
'I've found a map, let's have a blast!'
But the map is just leaves, oh what a tease,
They giggle together, looking for cheese.

A wise old owl hoots, with a chuckle and wink,
'In this leafy maze, you must really think.'
With every corner, a riddle anew,
'Is cheese out here, or is it just you?'

Under the sun, their laughter rolls,
In the leafy labyrinth, mischief controls.
With zest and spirit, they muse and roam,
Making legends of each twist, they call it home.

Portraits of the Pinecone Elder

In the woods, the pinecone swings,
With wisdom deep, he always sings.
His cap of green, a jaunty style,
Brings giggles forth and winsome smiles.

He tells of squirrels and acorn fights,
Of burly bears and funny sights.
With jokes so dry, they crack like logs,
He spins his tales 'tween laughing frogs.

The woodland critters, they gather 'round,
To hear his tales of wobbly sound.
Each nutty jest, a plucky cheer,
For in his shade, they gather near.

So raise a toast to this old sage,
Whose pinecone crown shall never age.
With every laugh upon the ground,
The spirit of the forest's found.

Rhymes of the Rivulet's Rush

Down by the brook, where bubbles giggle,
The waters dance, and pebbles wriggle.
With laughter bright, the fish do leap,
As frogs compete in splashy sweep.

The rivulet tells tales of glee,
Of adventurers lost in a tree.
With whimsy wide, it spins and whirls,
While dragonflies in laughter twirl.

It carries whispers of the breeze,
Of clumsy otters and buzzing bees.
Each ripple holds a joke retold,
As reeds in chorus, bold yet old.

So come and listen to the flow,
Where water sings and spirits glow.
In this giggling stream, joy runs deep,
As nature plays, and silence sleeps.

Murmurs of the Mystic Canopy

Up in the trees, where whispers play,
The leaves gossip through the day.
Each branch a jester, tall and spry,
With tales of clouds that tickle by.

The owls chuckle at moonlit pranks,
While shadows dance on leafy banks.
A squirrel's flip sends branches crack,
And laughter echoes, bouncing back.

Among the boughs, secrets peek,
A fox with wit, so sly and sleek.
With every rustle, a punchline waits,
As creatures giggle at their fates.

So join the dance in emerald green,
Where friendship blooms and joy is seen.
In this enchanted world so bright,
The canopy sings with sheer delight.

Dialogues with the Dappled Dawn

When morning breaks, the sun's a tease,
Waking flowers, stirring bees.
The dew drops twinkle, laughing clear,
As shadows dance, they jump with cheer.

The birds exchange their morning jokes,
While sneaky mice play with the blokes.
Each ray of light brings chuckles bright,
In this warm embrace of soft daylight.

The pretty petals wear a grin,
While butterflies flutter with a spin.
With giggling winds, they flit and soar,
Creating laughter forevermore.

So greet the dawn with open heart,
For every day's a brand new start.
In this playful world of joyful hues,
The morning laughs, igniting muse.

The Light Between the Underbrush.

In dappled light the critters dance,
A squirrel steals a glance,
With acorn hat and tiny shoes,
He twirls around, a nutty muse.

The rabbit sings a silly tune,
While frogs croak bass, beneath the moon,
A hedgehog plays a jazzy beat,
With tiny paws and rhythm neat.

The flowers laugh, the grass does sway,
As creatures join the grand ballet,
A waltzing mouse with twinkling eyes,
He jiggles by, a slight surprise.

When shadows stretch and daylight fades,
They take their bows, parade parades,
In every nook, a giggle grows,
In nature's play, everyone knows.

Echoes in the Fern

Beneath the fronds, a story spins,
A lizard grins, and mischief begins,
With sudden jumps, he starts a game,
While curly ferns just laugh his name.

A beetle boasts of brave exploits,
He flies around with all his might,
But trips and lands with quite a thud,
And giggles rise like springtime bud.

The owls laugh softly in the trees,
As night unfolds with playful tease,
They hoot a tune of jest and cheer,
For every critter swiftly near.

With echoes tangled in the ferns,
The woodland's heart forever churns,
In every rustle, laughter sings,
A symphony of silly things.

Whispers Beneath the Canopy

The branches sway, a secret told,
Of acorns dumb and tales of old,
A raccoon peeks with clever eyes,
He juggles fruits, to sweet surprise.

The wind carries a giggly breeze,
That tickles leaves and bends the trees,
In every whisper secrets gleam,
With bouncing hearts and drowsy dreams.

A tarantula with a top hat,
Insects cheer with a tip-tap spat,
He bows and sways in dandy style,
While butterflies grin all the while.

Beneath the canopy we find,
A playful world, a joyous mind,
Where every shout and gentle squawk,
Turns woodland paths to laughter's walk.

Moonlit Paths of the Thicket

Upon the paths of twinkling light,
The shadows frolic, brave the night,
With giggles rising, stars do wink,
As creatures plot in moonbeam ink.

A weasel wears a rosy scarf,
While singing sweetly, he can't help but laugh,
With every tune a lark appears,
Dancing round, shedding their fears.

The hoot of owls becomes a jest,
As fireflies join the swirling fest,
They twirl and swirl, what joyful sights,
A glowing dance that sparks delights.

In thickets thick where shadows play,
The lively throng will brightly stay,
With every step in merry cheer,
The night echoes, fun's drawing near.

Serenade of the Stream's Flow

Down by the river, a frog made a song,
He croaked out a note, loud and strong.
A fish leaped high, splashing his tune,
While dragonflies danced to the light of the moon.

Turtles wore hats, looking quite grand,
Discussing the weather, plotting their land.
A snail with a grin took a stroll near the bank,
Said, "Life's a race, yet I'm still in the plank!"

The waterbug spun like a dancer in sport,
Winking at minnows with a splashy retort.
While otters rolled in the grass so lush,
Laughing aloud at the river's sweet rush.

So come take a seat by the bubbling stream,
Join in the laughter, the joy, and the dream.
For nature's a stage with a vibrant show,
And every small creature knows where to go.

Reverie in the Remnant Woods

In the heart of the woods where the squirrels do prance,
There's a dance of the leaves, a whimsical dance.
The raccoons are plotting a mischievous scheme,
While owls exchange gossip, or so it would seem.

A bear found a hat, much too small for his head,
He strutted on by, 'I'm the king!' he said.
A chipmunk giggled, from a branch up above,
"That hat's not a crown, but you wear it with love!"

The trees hold their laughter, their branches a-shake,
As branches get tangled, oh what a mistake!
A porcupine laughed, rolling on a log,
At the sight of a turtle dressed up like a dog.

Under twilight's glow, everything's bright,
Nature's a circus, so pure and so light.
With critters all laughing in wild merry jest,
The woods aren't just quiet, they're lively the best!

The Call of the Cloven Hoof

In the midst of the fields, there's a goat with a plan,
He prances and leaps, quite proud of his span.
With a wink and a nod, he calls to the flock,
"Let's head to the barn for a wild donkey rock!"

A sheep shakes her wool and gives him a grin,
"But last time your dancing made all of us spin!"
The rooster laughed loud, stood tall on his post,
"Oh, goat, your balance is what I love most!"

With humor they gathered, the barn door flung wide,
And they all took their place for a barnyard joy ride.
As he twirled to the left, the chickens took flight,
The goat just fell over in sheer pure delight.

Their jubilee echoed, from dusk until dawn,
The barn came alive, each critter and brawn.
From mooing to clucks, the sounds filled the night,
In a world of their own, every heart felt the light.

Tales from the Timberline

At the edge of the woods where the tall pines sway,
A moose with a bow tie announced, "Let's play!"
He hosted a picnic with veggies and cheer,
As the critters all gathered, from far and near.

A rabbit arrived with a basket so neat,
Filled with fresh veggies, oh what a treat!
A bear brought some honey, just dripping and sweet,
While chipmunks brought brownies, quite hard to beat!

They shared funny stories of things gone astray,
Like the time that a crow flew away with their hay.
With laughter exploding, they danced round and round,
While the stream hummed along with a bubbling sound.

As the sun set low and the stars took their cue,
These tales from the timberline felt ever so true.
So raise a small glass made of bark and some leaves,
For friendships are golden, and humor conceives!

Notes of Nature's Nostalgia

In the woods, the squirrels play,
Chasing shadows, night and day.
A frog croaks out a silly song,
While crickets join, they sing along.

A rabbit hops with quite a flair,
Tripping on his floppy ear.
The trees crack jokes, the stars will wink,
Nature laughs as we all think.

The breezes tease the boughs and leaves,
Tickling whispers, nature weaves.
A toadstool wears a tiny hat,
Giggling harmlessly, imagine that!

Each dance and prance in moonlit glow,
Nature's stage, a charming show.
A nightingale with a comic tale,
Whispers secrets on the trail.

Verities in the Verdant Silence

Beneath the trees, a mouse recites,
Punning on the roots with might.
Dandelions giggle in the breeze,
While bees debate the taste of cheese.

Rustling leaves, a rusted tune,
As chipmunks plot beneath the moon.
A lizard slides with comic flair,
Practicing its stand-up dare.

Raccoons in masks form a band,
Playing spoons and clapping hands.
The thicket hums with laughter's sound,
As nature's humor does abound.

Blades of grass wear silly crowns,
While critters dance all around.
A woodland stage, without a care,
Filled with joy and laughter rare.

Fables from the Ferny Depth

In a glade where shadows play,
Frogs tell tales of a soggy day.
The mushrooms giggle, wearing spots,
As they list all of their plots.

A tiny bug makes quite a fuss,
Claiming royalty on the bus.
Grassy fields lay out their schemes,
In a world that's sewn from dreams.

Worms narrate with squiggly flair,
As hedgehogs prickily compare.
A dance of petals in the breeze,
Tickles noses and makes hearts tease.

The brook gurgles its funny tune,
Underneath a broad, bright moon.
Nature's laughter rings and sways,
In ferny nooks where joy displays.

Incantations of the Ivy

Up the wall, the ivy climbs,
Singing silly, twisted rhymes.
A snail whispers, slick with glee,
"As slow as me, you'll never see!"

The raccoon acts, a playful thief,
Stealing kisses from the leaf.
Owls roll their eyes and hoot with zest,
"Who knew ivy was so blessed?"

A swing of branches, vine and song,
Nature's jester dances along.
The shadows blush, both shy and sweet,
In this leafy land where laughter's neat.

With every giggle, roots entwine,
Stitching laughter into the pine.
A world where humor surely thrives,
And nature's joy forever jives.

Stories of the Woodland Shade

In the shade where shadows play,
Squirrels dance in bright ballet.
A fox sneezes—what a sight!
Leaves laugh and cheer in delight.

Frogs in crowns hop, bold and loud,
Claiming their throne, feeling proud.
A turtle winks with great finesse,
Promising tales of wilderness.

A rabbit in spectacles writes a book,
On how to avoid that tricky nook.
Chasing tails and spinning yarns,
The woods echo with friendly charms.

Secrets of the Wildflower Glen

In the glen where daisies giggle,
Bees tease flowers in a wiggle.
A butterfly claims it's a jet,
Zooming past, not one regret.

Rabbits plot a garden feast,
With carrots served by an eager beast.
They'll cook it up with a splash of fun,
And then they'll dance when all is done!

In sunlight's gaze, the petals grin,
Tickling bees who buzz and spin.
A secret pact, the blooms confess,
To dress the world in vibrant dress.

Lullabies of the Forest Floor

On the floor where critters sleep,
A snail dreams in a squishy heap.
Crickets chirp a sleepy tune,
Beneath the watchful gaze of the moon.

Woolly worms wear party hats,
Wiggling round like acrobats.
A blanket made of twigs and leaves,
Cradles whispering tales that weave.

Beneath the stars, the owlets coo,
As fireflies join in a twinkling crew.
Lullabies drift like gentle streams,
Carrying wishes into dreams.

Melodies among the Moss

In the moss where mushrooms sway,
Fungi dance like they're in a play.
A snail conducts with a leafy wand,
Guiding tunes of the forest's pond.

The wind hums low, a soft serenade,
While toadstools tap, dancing in the shade.
Bouncing beetles form a band,
Playing music across the land.

Every note is a giggle shared,
As woodland critters come prepared.
Underneath the twinkling stars,
The forest hums in joyful bars.

Dreaming in the Dappled Light

In the forest where shadows play,
The squirrels debate the best way.
They laugh as they leap from tree to tree,
While the bumblebees hum in harmony.

A rabbit wears glasses and reads a book,
Telling tales that make the owls look.
The fox takes notes with a quill in his paw,
As the kittens join in with a playful roar.

The sunbeams tease the leaves so bright,
Creating worlds of whimsical flight.
A deer, with a crown made of twigs,
Holds court as the woodland life jigs.

So dance with the shadows, embrace the delight,
In the laughter of nature, everything feels right.
With a wink and a nod, we take to the air,
Dreaming together without a care.

Songs of the Solstice Glade

Upon the hill where the lilies sway,
Frogs start singing, not far away.
They croak in chorus, a well-timed play,
While the crickets join in, no time to delay.

A hedgehog tap-dances, it's quite a sight,
With tiny top hat, he twirls with might.
The owls hoot softly, "What a fine night!"
As the fireflies twinkle, oh what a light!

A badger in boots leads a parade,
With all of his friends who are unafraid.
They prance and they twirl, none were delayed,
Making magic till the dawn was made.

So gather round under the starry dome,
In the glade of laughter, we all feel at home.
With songs and with smiles, we dance till we sway,
In this charming place, we wish time would stay.

Odyssey of the Orchard

Underneath the apple trees, folks roam,
Chasing after shadows, calling them home.
The wind whispers secrets, hearty and light,
As the pears hear tales from the stars at night.

An old raccoon wears a silly hat,
With a grin that says, "Let's have a chat!"
He offers sweet pies, made of pure bliss,
While the bees buzz around him, oh what a kiss!

The fruit's juicy laughter echoes around,
As cherries and plums dance on the ground.
A picnic of giggles, no worries found,
In this orchard of joy, love truly abounds.

So join in the mischief, let's make it last,
With glee in our hearts, we forget the past.
In a world filled with fun, so perfectly cast,
In this idyllic paradise, forever steadfast.

The Dance of the Dew-Kissed Blades

In the meadow where the daisies sway,
Grasshoppers bound in their merry play.
With tiny top hats and spectacles twink,
They prance on the blades, as the daisies wink.

A ladybug leads, with style and flair,
As butterflies flutter with color to share.
They twirl through the petals, skip through the air,
As the morning dew sparkles with flair.

The sun stretches out, spreading its rays,
Painting the world in warm golden bays.
Each laugh that escapes puts worries at bay,
In this dance of the greens, let's laugh and play.

So join the wild revel, let your heart soar,
In the light of the meadow, there's always more.
In the rhythm of life, with joy we explore,
In the dance of the blades, we ask for no more.

Whispers Among the Ferns

In the glade where ferns do sway,
Squirrels brag of acorn play.
They chatter, tease, and dance around,
While hidden gnomes prepare to clown.

A hedgehog wears a tiny hat,
And wonders just where the fish are at.
The rabbits giggle, tails askew,
As butterflies paint skies in hue.

A toad croaks jokes with such a flair,
While dragonflies spin tales in air.
Laughter echoes 'neath the leaves,
Where magic lives and no one grieves.

So come and join the playful throng,
Where nature sings its merry song.
In the ferns, you'll find delight,
A world of whimsy wrapped up tight.

Lament of the Woodland Shadows

The shadows play a game of hide,
In trunks of trees, they take their pride.
With silly faces, they make a show,
As night arrives, the mischief flows.

An owl hoots with dramatic flair,
As mice do breakdance without a care.
A raccoon giggles, paws full of snacks,
While the moonlight gives its silver tracks.

Each wind gust brings a chuckle or two,
As leaves gossip like the best of a crew.
In whispers soft, they tease and taunt,
As the stars above begin to vaunt.

But don't mistake their playful jest,
In shadows deep, they take a rest.
And in the dark, the laughter stays,
A secret kept through night and days.

The Echoes Beneath the Canopy

Beneath the leaves where sunlight breaks,
The whispers weave like funny flakes.
A chipmunk juggles acorns with glee,
While the bees buzz in harmony.

The raccoons hold wild parties at dusk,
With berries and honey, it's quite the task.
They dance to the rhythm of nature's tune,
Under the watch of a captivated moon.

A parrot perched, with pranks up its sleeve,
Repeats the snickers of those who believe.
The echoing laughter rings through the trees,
A symphony stirred by the softest breeze.

So listen closely, delight in the sound,
Of woodland antics that swirl all around.
For in every rustle, a chuckle can bloom,
Beneath the green canopy, joy finds its room.

Twilight Serenade in the Thicket

In twilight's glow, the thicket wakes,
With silly critters plotting pranks and shakes.
A badger strums on a twig for flair,
While frogs croak tunes with a wild air.

The fireflies waltz, twinkling bright,
As the hedgehog leads the dance tonight.
Each giggle ripples through the soft grass,
In this charming thicket where time will pass.

A fox tells tales of daring deeds,
To a crowd of friends who find their seeds.
With every chuckle, the stars shine more,
As laughter mingles with the night's soft roar.

So as the evening wraps you tight,
Remember to smile at nature's light.
In thickets deep, may joy be found,
Where every creature leaps and bounds.

Songs of the Silent Glade

In the glade where whispers play,
Dancing shadows steal the day.
Squirrels chatter, loud and clear,
They've a gossiping squirrel here!

Mice play hide and seek at night,
In the moon's soft, silvery light.
Crickets sing a tune so sweet,
While the frogs tap dance on their feet.

A lazy hare, he tells a jest,
Of garden vegetables, the best.
And though the fox plots a sneak,
He trips on roots, and oh, how bleak!

Larks burst forth with laughter bright,
As breezes carry them in flight.
In the glade where fun abounds,
Joyful echoes fill the sounds.

Vows Among the Vines

Amidst the grapes, a pledge they make,
Two snails toast with a piece of cake.
With shells all polished, they declare,
A love that's slower—without a care!

Bumblebees buzz with glee,
Trading honey like it's free.
From flower beds, a baker's dream,
Where petals join, all burst with cream.

Worms entwined, they dig and sigh,
In soil deep, beneath the sky.
Roses giggle at their vows,
While daisies dance and take their bows.

The sun sets low, the moon will rise,
Vows whispered under starlit skies.
United in laughter, they hold the line,
In the vineyards where joys entwine.

Dreams of the Elderflower

In dreams, the elderflower sways,
With visions sweet of sunny days.
A rabbit dreams of endless greens,
While birds plan parties, it seems!

Beneath the blooms, there's quite a chat,
Of beetles dressed in dapper hats.
The butterflies are all aflutter,
Debating where to spread their butter!

A fox rolls in a field of gold,
Pledging mischief, brave and bold.
But dreams can twist, like tangled vines,
As cats on roofs write silly lines.

With every petal, laughter grows,
In the world where humor flows.
Elderflower's dreams take flight,
Bringing chuckles through the night.

Soliloquy of the Still Woods

In woods so still, a squirrel speaks,
Of acorn plans and hide-and-seeks.
The trees nod slow, they're in on the fun,
As sunbeams play till the day is done.

A wise old owl hoots with a grin,
"Who's got the best tales, let's begin!"
With every croak, the frogs reply,
Their heavy accents make the time fly!

A raccoon shares a pie he stole,
Echoes of laughter, the grandest goal.
As whispers weave through branches tight,
The woods hold secrets of every plight.

In this soliloquy of cheer,
Nature's jesters gather near.
With every crack of limb and bough,
The woods reveal their laughter now.

The Chronicles of the Swaying Alder

In the breeze the alders dance,
Their branches waving like a prance.
Frogs break into a song so loud,
While beetles form a funky crowd.

Squirrels wear their silly hats,
Pretending they're the coolest cats.
The sun dips low, a golden hue,
And tree trunks start to groove anew.

Leaves have parties after dark,
With fireflies to add a spark.
They twirl and spin, what a sight,
All through the cool and starry night.

So come and join this woodland fun,
Where laughter stretches like a bun.
The swaying alder leads the way,
In this amusing, leafy ballet.

Serenade of the Autumn Leaves

The autumn's here, the leaves conspire,
To start a dance that won't expire.
They whirl around with giggles sweet,
And kick up clouds beneath your feet.

A leaf fell down, it wobbled wide,
It took a tumble, what a ride!
With every gust and gusty cheer,
They plan a prank on us right here.

The trees all laugh, they shade their eyes,
As swirling leaves wear silly ties.
They've got a rhythm, can't you see?
A concert beneath the old oak tree.

With trumpets made of acorn shells,
The woodland band performs quite well.
So let us sway, with roots interlaced,
In autumn's song, we're all embraced.

The Lullaby of the Ancient Roots

Beneath the soil, the roots do snore,
As creatures play and make much more.
A hedgehog hums a gentle tune,
While moles are plotting in the gloom.

Old roots can tell the funniest tales,
Of odd little critters and their fails.
How rabbits struggled to hop and grin,
And danced 'til dusk with a toothy spin.

The groundhog rolls, a playful beast,
While gnarled roots just laugh, at least.
A snoozy fox joins in the throng,
This lullaby won't last too long.

So listen close, beneath the trees,
To whispers shared upon the breeze.
In roots we find a cozy humor,
The land's own grinning little rumor.

Folklore of the Gnarled Trees

Beneath the gnarled branches great,
Lies folklore that's simply first-rate.
The trees swap stories, root to root,
   About the squirrel keeping suit.

One claims the owls wear tiny hats,
Others argue 'bout the chubby bats.
The winds just giggle, swirling 'round,
   Adding laughs to the wooded sound.

As acorns chuckle on the ground,
A wise old oak plays the clown around.
With laughter echoing through the glades,
   In tales of joy, their folly wades.

So gather 'round, you merry friends,
   The lore of trees, it never ends.
With roots entwined, we'll dream tonight,
In gnarled branches, everything's alright.

Tales from the Undergrowth

In the thicket where squirrels prance,
A rabbit lost his pants!
He searched high, he searched low,
But found only a snouty crow.

The hedgehogs had a tea party spree,
With acorn cups for all who see.
They laughed as they soaked their tiny toes,
While the bumblebees hummed sweet prose.

A tortoise slow, in a hurry to race,
Challenged the hare, oh what a case!
But fell asleep beneath a fern,
And dreamt of treats at every turn.

A frog in a bowler, such a sight,
Sang loudly to the moon so bright.
The fireflies flickered, lost in glee,
As he croaked of his dreams by the old oak tree.

Sighs of the Swaying Branches

Under branches that carelessly sway,
A parrot mimics what others say.
'The cat is a hat, and the grass is a shoe!'
The rabbits declared, 'Oh, what is true?'

The leaves whisper tales of grand charades,
Of dancing twigs and bright escapades.
An owl with glasses reads out loud,
While the rabbits gather, laughing proud.

A group of bugs with tiny guitars,
Strummed to the rhythm of passing cars.
They sang of pollen and sweet summer nights,
Creating a concert beneath the lights.

A curious fox, in a top hat so fine,
Joined in the fun with dance so divine.
And all of the forest clapped in delight,
As the sun waved goodbye, bidding goodnight.

Chronicles of the Verdant Vale

In the vale where the daisies grow tall,
A pig in a tutu decided to squall.
With a twirl and a swiney flair,
He called for the creatures to gather and stare.

The badger brought cookies, quite round and sweet,
While the fox served punch with a rhythmic beat.
The raccoons brought spoons, shiny and bright,
For a feast in the woods under the moonlight.

A shy little turtle came late to the scene,
Wore a crown made of leaves, and felt like a queen.
She danced with the birds, and spun in the grass,
Declaring her reign would forever last.

With giggles and chuckles, the night went ahead,
As tales of mischief filled each creature's head.
And swaying to tunes of a merry old tale,
The night became magic down in the vale.

Harmony of the Hidden Grove

In the grove where the shadows play tricks,
A raccoon played chess with some clever chicks.
The stakes were some berries, sweet as could be,
But the chick was too cunning, so clever, you see!

The mice held a party with cheese galore,
While the owls spun yarns of the days before.
Each whisper and giggle drifted on air,
As the elves painted colors with delicate care.

A squirrel in disco gear started to dance,
With moves that could put any fox in a trance.
The trees all bobbed, with leaves in a whirl,
As laughter erupted from every boy and girl.

As the twilight faded, the fun didn't end,
The rabbit's tall tales made hearts twist and bend.
With hugs all around, and wee ones in tow,
They celebrated joy in the hidden grove's glow.

Verses from the Secret Glens

In a glen where whispers play,
And mushrooms dance without delay,
A squirrel stole a pie today,
And made the rabbits shout, "Hooray!"

With sneaky paws, he made his claim,
The forest critters joined the game,
They turned the glen into a fame,
Where food and fun were both the same.

A fox came in to try and tease,
But tripped on roots, fell with the trees,
The laugh erupted, if you please,
As everyone sat down for cheese.

So if you hear a chuckle loud,
Amidst the trees, a merry crowd,
Remember in the bracken proud,
They feast and frolic, nature's shroud.

The Gossamer Thread of Twilight

Twilight's gossamer threads unfurl,
As fireflies begin to whirl,
A rabbit sports a tiny pearl,
That's gotten lost in her soft curl.

The hedgehog wears a hat askew,
While owl hoots, "What shall we do?"
A dance-off starts, much to pursue,
While crickets play a tune or two.

The stars above roll their bright eyes,
As bunnies bounce and send up sighs,
Each stumble met with sweet surprise,
Under the twinkling, cheering skies.

So join the jests beneath the shade,
Where twilight's magic is displayed,
With giggles shared and none dismayed,
The merriment will never fade.

A Reverie Among the Pines

In pines where secrets whisper low,
And mischievous breezes twist and blow,
A goat tried dancing, stole the show,
By tripping on a stub, oh no!

The birds all chirped, "Let's start a crew!"
They flocked to join, with feathers new,
A conga line began to brew,
With hops and skips, a lively cue.

A badger blushed, he grabbed a stick,
Pretending it was magic, slick,
But fell upon a tangle, quick,
And laughed so hard, it made him sick!

So in the pines, where antics bloom,
And laughter chases away the gloom,
Each day offers a joyful room,
In nature's heart, we find our zoom!

Murmurs of the Dappled Path

On dappled paths where shadows lie,
A hedgehog rolled, oh my, oh my!
He hid from laughter, fancied sly,
While giggling flowers waved him by.

The toads held court with crowns of leaves,
Debating who could dance in eves,
With clumsy moves that no one believes,
Their croaks and hops are true reprieves.

A group of ants claimed they would sing,
To serenade the bees in spring,
But all they did was flap and fling,
In jumbled harmony, they cling!

So wander down that path of cheer,
Where each odd sight brings laughter near,
The whispers of the woods sincere,
Shall fill your heart with joy and cheer!

Legends of the Leafy Realm

In a kingdom of trees where the squirrels plot,
A raccoon in boots plays a prank that's hot.
He juggles some acorns, he dances with flair,
While the owls just hoot, wondering how to care.

The ferns gossip wildly, they twist and they sway,
Telling tales of a fox who's lost his own way.
With a hat made of leaves and a grin so wide,
He prances around like he's got nothing to hide.

Yet the mushrooms mutter, 'What's all this fuss?'
While the daisies laugh, gathering round in a rush.
With petals aflutter, they join in the fun,
As the rabbits perform as if they have won.

But when the moon glows with a silver delight,
The creatures all gather, their hearts feeling light.
Together they chuckle beneath starlit streams,
In the legends of leaves, all is laughter and dreams.

Rhythms of the Rooted Earth

Underneath the ground where the worms like to groove,
The beetles are spinning and trying to prove.
With a tap of their legs and a wiggle so spry,
They dance for the roots, raising laughs to the sky.

A porcupine strummed on a branch made of reeds,
While the slugs formed a band playing songs full of leads.
Though slow with their rhythm, they keep on the beat,
And the moles dig the sound with their wiggly feet.

The crickets are crooning, the frogs join in too,
They harmonize sweetly as night breezes blew.
Yet the shadows keep sneaking, with giggles and grins,
As the grasshoppers leap where the laughter begins.

With a wiggle and a jiggle, the party is grand,
Underneath the soil, in their green, leafy land.
The rhythms of roots sing an upbeat refrain,
In a world where the funny blooms plentifully again.

Sonnet to the Solitary Pine

Oh, solitary pine, what a sight you must see,
With a needle-like crown, swaying light and free.
You ponder the jokes that the breeze likes to tell,
Of the hiccuping saplings who grow way too well.

You whisper to critters who scamper around,
Sharing giggles and secrets beneath your vast crown.
While the winds make you waltz, you smile with delight,
Watching all the antics from morning till night.

But tell me, dear pine, do you ever feel blue,
When the shadows get longer and days start to skew?
Perhaps you just chuckle, rustling your leaves,
As the squirrels make faces, pulling on their sleeves.

So here's to the moments of whims you bestow,
With laughter and cheer that you always bestow.
In your branches, there's magic, no need for a shrine,
For a tree who can giggle is truly divine.

Ghosts in the Greenery

In the thicket at twilight, strange sights appear,
With ghosts made of vines whispering jokes in your ear.
They float through the ferns causing mischief and fright,
While the bugs roll their eyes at bizarre ghostly sights.

They twirl and they tumble, a spectral parade,
Playing hopscotch on leaves in their leafy charade.
With a flap and a flounce, they invite you to play,
Though the frightened old hedgehogs just scurry away.

The trees shake with laughter at the antics around,
As the gnomes hide their faces, not making a sound.
While the fog plays the music, eerie yet bright,
These ghosts in the greenery dance through the night.

But you needn't be scared, for they come without harm,
Just to tickle your toes and bring merry to charm.
With their laughter lingering, like dew on a seed,
They haunt with a humor that all hearts must heed.

Sonnet of the Wandering Breeze

A breeze danced past with such delight,
It tickled trees, both day and night.
It whispered jokes to flowers bright,
And made the leaves giggle in flight.

The butterflies laughed, they couldn't keep still,
As the wind spun tales over the hill.
The clouds rolled in, all fluffy and round,
Joining the jest, adding to the sound.

Yet even the gust had its hiccoughs and farts,
Sending spindly branches into fits of starts.
Squirrels were flustered, chasing their tails,
While butterflies blushed in their colorful veils.

Oh, merry breeze with your playful tease,
You're the jester of woods, a dance on the knees.
In a world full of whispers and chuckles so grand,
You bring laughter with every gust at hand.

Enchanted Grove Melodies

In the grove where critters convene,
The frogs croak out tunes, a quirky scene.
They hop and they croon with such glee,
While raccoons join in with wild jubilee.

A squirrel with style, in a top hat and tie,
Sings 'swing low, sweet chariot,' oh my!
A deer taps its hooves on the mossy floor,
As crickets provide the beat, wanting more.

The confused owl just turns and asks,
'Can someone please share their dancing masks?'
But all he gets is a laugh in reply,
Heavin' that brow, as if to oh why?

As day fades and stars start to gleam,
The melodies linger, in a whimsical dream.
Each rustle and giggle, the night they will sway,
In this merry grove, forever they'll play.

A Song for the Swaying Grasses

The grasses sway, a zany parade,
Tickled by breezes, they dance unafraid.
A chorus of whispers, they giggle and chat,
Each blade with a tale, how about that!

One tells of a snail who lost his way,
While another claims a spider can play.
They gossip of daisies who think they are stars,
And regale of the rabbit who stole their guitars!

As evening descends, the fireflies blink,
With rhythm that makes even the frogs think.
Each flicker a note, each movement a song,
The grasses all trumpet, "We've danced all along!"

So if ever you wander where the tall grasses sway,
Remember their laughter at the end of the day.
For in this green sea, joy can be found,
In the sway and the wiggle, laughter abounds.

Legends Woven in Moss

In the cool shade where stories grow,
Moss weaves tales in a humorous flow.
Legends of toads who wore tiny shoes,
And a snail in a cloak making funny news.

A weasel once thought he was quite a knight,
Challenging spiders to dance in the night.
But he tripped on a log, oh what a sight,
Came tumbling down with a comical fright!

The wise old owl, with glasses askew,
Says, "Don't mind the blunders, they're part of the view!"

As chipmunks compose a merry refrain,
To liven the forest and banish the pain.

So gather ye round, hear the mossy lore,
Of critters and antics and fun evermore.
In each twist and curl, with laughter we find,
The joy of the woods, with humor entwined.

Tales of the Loamy Earth

In the garden where gnomes play,
With carrots that dance in the day,
The rabbits wear hats made of hay,
While worms sing a tune, oh so gay.

A snail on a leaf took a ride,
With a ladybug acting as guide,
They laughed at the beetles who tried,
To boast of their speed, then they cried.

A cabbage waved hello with glee,
And onions made quite a sight, you see,
The radishes joined in the spree,
As the soil held a party, carefree.

So if you stroll through this realm of green,
Expect the unexpected, it's keen,
For laughter echoes, bright and serene,
In the loamy earth, life's a scene!

Mysteries in the Misty Hollow

In the hollow where shadows may creep,
Lived a squirrel who couldn't keep,
His acorns straight, oh what a heap,
He'd trip on his stash, in a leap!

The owls told jokes that fell flat,
While the raccoons danced in a hat,
The toads held a ball, imagine that,
With croaking tunes and a tap-tap!

Fog rolled in like an old, friendly ghost,
Filling the air with laughter's boast,
A fox joined the fun, at the most,
As shadows danced, raising a toast!

So venture where the mist leaves a trace,
With tricks and pranks in every place,
The world is a stage, full of space,
Where giggles and laughter embrace!

The Dance of the Boughs

When the wind gave the branches a shake,
The trees started to jig, what a quake!
Leaves flittered down, like confetti cake,
While squirrels took part, for fun's sake.

A woodpecker drummed, keeping beat,
As the dance floor joined in, quite neat,
With mushrooms all clapping their feet,
And hedgehogs rolled in, feeling sweet!

The brook nearby chimed in with a splish,
While frogs croaked a tune, quite a dish,
The flowers swayed, fulfilling their wish,
For dance in the woods, oh so swish!

So next time you hear the trees sway,
Join in their dance, don't just stay,
For nature's a party, come what may,
With joy and laughter leading the way!

Hymn of the Serpent Stream

In the stream where the fish love to play,
A serpent sways in a charming way,
It tickles the frogs, brightening their day,
While minnows wiggle in a ballet.

With a splash and a dive, oh what a show,
The otters glide with a twist and a flow,
While turtles wear glasses, feeling quite so,
As the banks of the stream cheer with a glow!

Dragonflies twirl, sending whispers of glee,
They'd land on the nose of a grumpy old bee,
Who chased them away, but with laughter, you see,
Nature's mishaps are wild and carefree.

So wander beside that cheerful stream,
Where moments are bright, and giggles beam,
With jesters and dancers, life's a dream,
In the flow of the water's whimsical theme!

Reflections in the Ribbed Bark

In the forest, trees all grin,
Swaying softly, where to begin?
Bark like wrinkled old men's skin,
Tickled by breezes, where we spin.

Squirrels chatter, each silly tale,
Dancing 'round without a fail.
Hiding nuts beneath their trail,
While the owls hoot, 'O' what a gale!'

Raccoons debate who takes the prize,
As the critters share their wise lies.
Laughter echoes 'neath the skies,
Nature's jesters in sweet disguise.

Frogs croak loudly, join the fun,
Jumping higher, they've just begun.
In this jest, we are all one,
A merry dance 'til day is done.

Verses of the Verdant Vista

Green hills roll with a chuckle bright,
Where the daisies dance in pure delight.
Bumbles buzz in a wobbly flight,
Chasing shadows, oh what a sight!

A goat on a hill, munching grass high,
With a bleat that sounds like a silly sigh.
Rolling down, oh me, oh my!
A tumbleweed's laugh, as it waves goodbye.

Pine needles drop, a gentle tease,
How they pirouette in the warm breeze.
The sun peeks, wearing his golden keys,
Joking around with the buzzing bees.

Chirping birds craft witty refrains,
With melodies echoing in their veins.
The vibrant green, where laughter reigns,
In this playful world, joy never wanes.

Anecdotes of the Acorn's Fall

An acorn dropped from a lofty perch,
Tumbled down from its sturdy church.
"Oh dear tree, you've led me to search,"
As squirrels roll in their woodland lurch.

Rabbits giggle, hopping on by,
Their wiggly tails waving a sly goodbye.
In the sight of an owl, who dared to spy,
"Stop that laughing, or I'll surely cry!"

Leaves rustle softly, gossip and chat,
Spilling secrets of the wise little bat.
"What's next for our hero, the brave acorn brat?"
"Perhaps a tree, or a nest, or a mat?"

The woods alive with each silly tale,
Friendship blooms, as they set sail.
In the realm of wonder, they shall prevail,
Laughter echoing over hill and vale.

Cries of the Crow in the Copse

A crow sat perched with a caw so loud,
Hollering tales to a curious crowd.
"Listen close, for I'm wise and proud,
Fear not the fog, just say it out loud!"

With antics played on a branch so thin,
He juggles nuts with a cheeky grin.
The rabbits join in, have a good spin,
"Join the fun, let the laughter begin!"

"Come share a snack, let's steal some bread,
For a feast with my friends, we're all well-fed!"
As the sun starts to set, they dance instead,
A chorus of crows amidst laughter spread.

So when in the wood and you hear that caw,
Know there's a party, an informal law.
In the copse where the fun is never a flaw,
Life is a giggle, that's all we saw!

www.ingramcontent.com/pod-product-compliance
Lightning Source LLC
Chambersburg PA
CBHW071823160426
43209CB00003B/179